My School

Katie Peters

GRL Consultant Diane Craig,
Certified Literacy Specialist

Pull Ahead READERS

Lerner Publications ◆ Minneapolis

Note from a GRL Consultant
This Pull Ahead leveled book has been carefully designed for beginning readers. A team of guided reading literacy experts has reviewed and leveled the book to ensure readers pull ahead and experience success.

Lerner Publications
An imprint of Lerner Publishing Group, Inc.
241 First Avenue North
Minneapolis, MN 55401 USA

For reading levels and more information, look up this title at www.lernerbooks.com.

Main body text set in Memphis Pro 24/39
Typeface provided by Linotype.

Photo Acknowledgments
The images in this book are used with the permission of: © talevr/iStockphoto, p. 3; © ESB Professional/Shutterstock Images, pp. 4–5; © Wavebreakmedia/iStockphoto, pp. 6–7, 16 (teacher); © Air Images/Shutterstock Images, pp. 8–9; © New Africa/Shutterstock Images, pp. 10–11, 16 (apple); © FatCamera/iStockphoto, pp. 12–13, 16 (book); © Monkey Business Images/Shutterstock Images, pp. 14–15.

Front cover: © skynesher/iStockphoto

Library of Congress Cataloging-in-Publication Data

Names: Peters, Katie, author.
Title: My school / Katie Peters ; GRL Consultant Diane Craig, Certified Literacy Specialist.
Description: Minneapolis, MN : Lerner Publications, [2023] | Series: My world (Pull ahead readers - nonfiction) | Includes index. | Audience: Ages 4–7 | Audience: Grades K–1 | Summary: "This nonfiction title features carefully leveled text and engages readers with photographs of schools. Pairs with the fiction book Amana at School"— Provided by publisher.
Identifiers: LCCN 2022006209 (print) | LCCN 2022006210 (ebook) | ISBN 9781728475981 (library binding) | ISBN 9781728478906 (paperback) | ISBN 9781728483900 (ebook)
Subjects: LCSH: Schools—Juvenile literature.
Classification: LCC LB1513 .P43 2023 (print) | LCC LB1513 (ebook) | DDC 371—dc23

LC record available at https://lccn.loc.gov/2022006209
LC ebook record available at https://lccn.loc.gov/2022006210

Manufactured in the United States of America
1 – CG – 12/15/22

Table of Contents

My School

My school has classrooms.

1+1=2
2+2=

My school has teachers.

My school has a gym.

My school has a cafeteria.

My school has a library.

My school is fun!

What do you like best about your school?

Did You See It?

apple

book

teacher

Index